TERRORIST ATTACKS

THE ATTACK ON THE USS *COLE* IN YEMEN ON OCTOBER 12, 2000

Betty Burnett, Ph.D.

The Rosen Publishing Group, Inc.
New York

For Sam Dayball

Published in 2003 by The Rosen Publishing Group, Inc.
29 East 21st Street, New York, NY 10010

Library of Congress Cataloging-in-Publication Data

Burnett, Betty, 1940–
The attack on the USS *Cole* in Yemen on October 12, 2000 / by Betty Burnett.— 1st ed.
   p. cm. — (Terrorist attacks)
Summary: Describes the terrorist attack on the USS *Cole*, a destroyer whose UN mission was to patrol the northern Persian Gulf, as well as the aftermath, investigation, and context of the bombing.
Includes bibliographical references and index.
ISBN 0-8239-3860-3 (library binding)
1. *Cole* (Ship)—Juvenile literature. 2. USS *Cole* Bombing Incident, Aden, Yemen, 2000—Juvenile literature. 3. Terrorism—Yemen—Juvenile literature. 4. Terrorism—United States—Juvenile literature. 5. Bombing investigation—Yemen—Juvenile literature. 6. Yemen—Foreign relations—United States—Juvenile literature. 7. United States—Foreign relations—Yemen—Juvenile literature. [1. *Cole* (Ship) 2. USS *Cole* Bombing Incident, Aden, Yemen, 2000. 3. Terrorism. 4. Bombing investigation. 5. Yemen—Foreign relations—United States. 6. United States—Foreign relations—Yemen.]
I. Title. II. Series.
VA65.C57 B87 2003
953.35—dc21

2002010849

Manufactured in the United States of America

CONTENTS

INTRODUCTION

The Arabian Peninsula is bordered by the Red Sea to the west, the Gulf of Aden and the Indian Ocean to the south, and the Gulf of Oman and the Persian Gulf to the east. Across the Red Sea is Africa.

This region has dozens of "high-threat points" for potential violence and terrorism, according to the U.S. State Department. The Department of Defense has tagged it an Area of Responsibility (AOR) and charged the U.S. Central Command (USCENTCOM) with monitoring it and protecting U.S. interests there. Gen. Tommy Franks, USCENTCOM commander in chief, calls the area "very dangerous."

The AOR stretches more than 3,100 miles (4,988 km) east to west and 3,600 miles (5,792 km) north to south, a larger area than the continental United States. About a half billion people live in the AOR. They come from a variety of ethnic and religious backgrounds, but the language is primarily Arabic and the religion mainly Muslim.

Famine, drought, disease, and deep poverty characterize much of the region. With few educational opportunities and a high unemployment rate, many young people see their only hope for the future in extremist organizations. These extremist groups promise young people that their lives will be better once the Western world has no more power.

But the area contains great resources, such as oil, copper, iron, and gold. In today's global network, it is important to the world economy to keep open air lanes and sea-lanes, especially critical maritime "choke points," which could block the shipping of resources. One important choke point is Bab el Mandeb, a strait off the Yemen coast that connects the Red Sea and the Gulf of Aden. The United States needs to keep on friendly terms with Yemen to keep the choke point open.

The U.S. Navy's Central Command, NAVCENT, is in charge of all naval operations in the AOR. The United States maintains forces in the area to encourage a stable political situation, to keep the sea-lanes open, and to slow down aggression on the part of any nation against any other. The presence of navy ships reminds the AOR of American power and strength.

By staying in international waters away from land, NAVCENT vessels can operate freely, without requiring permission from sovereign nations. Surveillance airplanes must receive permission to fly over a nation. Without permission, they may be seen as enemies and attacked. Navy vessels on the open sea do not need this kind of permission.

By providing a continuous naval presence in the Red Sea, Gulf of Aden, and Persian Gulf, the United States hopes to prevent war. In case war is declared, the ships are ready for combat.

On August 8, 2000, a destroyer named the USS *Cole* left Norfolk, Virginia, to join the USS *George Washington* aircraft carrier battle group in the NAVCENT task force. The group's mission was to patrol the northern Persian Gulf.

The USS *Cole* is an Arleigh Burke–class, guided-missile destroyer, heavily armored and capable of attacking targets on land and sea.

THE USS COLE

The destroyer USS *Cole* was commissioned on June 8, 1996, in a ceremony at Port Everglades near Fort Lauderdale, Florida. It was a ship the navy was very proud of, an Arlcigh Burke–class destroyer, DDG 67: Flight I. Its price tag was $1 billion.

Destroyers are medium-sized ships, half as big as aircraft carriers, larger than submarines. The USS *Cole* measures 505 feet (154 meters) long and weighs 8,300 tons (7,529 metric tons). Destroyers are built to handle many operations at once. They can attack submarines, surface ships, and aircraft at the same time. In 1997, the Arleigh Burkes was

The USS *Cole* was named for Sgt. Darrell Samuel Cole, U.S. Marine Corps Reserve, who was awarded the Medal of Honor after his death for heroic action while fighting the Japanese on Iwo Jima in 1945. Cole destroyed two enemy emplacements with hand grenades, then, armed with only a pistol and hand grenades, attacked the enemy position, allowing his company to continue their advance.

equipped with the highest of high-tech weaponry.

Four gas-powered turbines, each rated at 33,600 hp, propel the *Cole* through the water. The turbines drive two shafts at 3,600 rpm. The propeller on each shaft can be moved to various positions as needed, allowing it to maneuver smoothly. At sea, the ship can maintain speeds in excess of 30 knots.

The *Cole* was designed to survive combat. It has an all-steel construction, and its most important areas are protected by two layers of steel and 70 tons (63.5 metric tons) of Kevlar armor, the strongest materials available for a ship. Kevlar armor is the material used in bulletproof vests.

The USS *Cole* is a floating version of a naval base. It has several decks below the top deck with offices and living quarters that provide workspace, comfortable staterooms, and areas for recreation. On the top deck is a platform where combat helicopters can land while they are refueling or being refitted with weapons. But unlike other ships, the *Cole* does not have a hangar to house a helicopter.

The most important equipment on an Arleigh Burke–class destroyer is the Aegis Combat System. This top-of-the-line security system integrates the ship's sensors and weapons systems. It takes information from radar, sonar, and satellite connections and relays it to the weapons on the ship to prepare them for firing. The Aegis system has four subsystems:

Sensors: The AN/SPY1 radar scans in all directions at once to find and track aircraft or missiles. It continuously watches the sky for new targets, from the horizon to the stratosphere. A bow-mounted AN/SQR 5C3 sonar continually monitors the ocean.

Assessment: The Command and Decision System (CDS) takes information from the sensors and prepares it in a form to be read by technicians. It can determine if a threat exists and how serious the threat is. It can also give information on what to do about it.

Presentation: The Aegis Display System (ADS) displays information important to the defense of the ship using material gathered by the sensors and processed by the CDS.

Deployment: The Weapons Control System (WCS) receives instruction from the CDS if the ship is threatened, then selects the weapons to use in its defense. It interfaces with the controls that fire the weapons. It is the system that actually "pulls the trigger."

All this information is relayed to computer terminals below deck where technicians monitor the screens twenty-four hours per day.

The weapons systems include Harpoon missiles for sea-to-sea combat and Tomahawk missiles for sea-to-land combat. The MK missile-launching system can fire a combination of up to ninety surface-to-air, surface-to-land, or surface-to-surface missiles from the deck of the ship. The antisubmarine missiles are launched vertically—straight down. There are also thirty-two torpedo tubes and a five-inch rapid-fire deck gun.

When the USS *Cole* left the naval base in Virginia, it was armed for anything any traditional enemy could throw at it.

The Crew

On board the *Cole* in the summer of 2000 were 249 men and 44 women. Many were on their first mission, some were new high school graduates still in their teens. The average age was twenty-two. Some crew members wanted to make a career of the navy, and others planned to use the navy training programs as a way to launch a civilian career. Some had joined the navy just "to see the world," as the old recruiting posters promised. Most of the sailors were technicians trained in high-tech warfare. All had been assigned specific jobs, from cook to engineer.

Commander Kirk Lippold, a Nevada native, was the captain. He had twenty years' experience in the navy. The

At the end of a fourteen-month restoration project, sailors line up on the deck of the USS *Cole* to watch a ceremony held in honor of the ship and its crew.

executive officer (XO) was Lt. Commander Chris Peterschmidt. After receiving a master of science degree in physics, Peterschmidt had worked on several ships and had been awarded the Navy Commendation Medal three times. It was his job to see that the captain's orders were followed.

The Route

When the *Cole* left Norfolk, Virginia, for the Persian Gulf on August 8, it headed south-southeast. For several weeks it cruised in the Atlantic Ocean holding drills while the crew became familiar with the ship and its equipment. The crew took the time to learn to work together smoothly as a team.

A tremendous number of the U.S.'s naval vessels, both active and inactive, are located in the Southeast. Here, tugboats guide a retired vessel, the Navy Landing Ship Dock (LSD) *Spiegel Grove*, away from its mooring at the James River Reserve Fleet at Fort Eustis, Virginia.

General Tommy Franks explained: "She was in workup—preparing plans, exercising in the Atlantic, and then once she was certified combat ready or ready to deploy by COM second fleet, then she moved from our East Coast into the European command area in the Mediterranean."

Once it was under way, the ship did not stop until it reached the port city of Barcelona, Spain, where it refueled. Next it stopped at points along the French Riviera and at the island of Malta. Then it moved through the Suez Canal in Egypt into the Red Sea.

The route from the Suez Canal through the Red Sea into the northern Persian Gulf is about 3,400 miles (5,470 km), farther than the ship could go without refueling. By the time the *Cole* got halfway along on that journey, at Aden, Yemen, the ship's gas tanks were expected to be a little more than 50 percent full. The *Cole* needed to travel another 1,800 miles (2,896 km) or so to its destination, so it was determined that Aden was a good place to refuel.

The Mission

The *Cole* was scheduled to take part in a Maritime Interception Operation (MIO) as part of a group effort that enforces the United Nations (UN) Security Council sanctions against Iraq. Specifically, its job was to monitor merchant vessel traffic in the Persian Gulf. Fifteen nations take part in this operation to enforce the UN prohibition on cargo originating from Iraq (especially oil) and any imports to Iraq that arrive without UN authorization.

The *Cole* was on a routine mission, one that would last for only a few months. The ship's commander had received no briefing on a specific danger in the area. He expected nothing out of the ordinary; he certainly did not expect combat. The ship was scheduled to return home on December 21.

Lacking modern military weapons, Palestinians throw rocks at Israeli troops, who have occupied the West Bank and Gaza Strip for years.

THREAT CONDITION BRAVO

CHAPTER 2

Palestinian leaders called Friday, October 6, 2000, a "day of rage." On that day, the beginning of the Jewish holy days of Yom Kippur, Israel sealed off the West Bank and Gaza Strip, keeping Muslim Palestinians from attending their midday prayers at the Al-Aqsa Mosque in Jerusalem. The act followed a week of Palestinian unrest and sporadic violence.

After learning that they wouldn't be allowed to go to the mosque, militant Islamic groups called for retaliation with any weapon at hand—rocks, guns, or bombs. In response, heavily armed Israeli tanks patrolled the area.

Several countries in the AOR rallied behind the angry Palestinians.

In Damascus, Syria, a mob gathered outside the U.S. Embassy to protest the United States's support of Israel. There was also a pro-Palestinian, anti-Israeli demonstration in Beirut, Lebanon. In Iraq, thousands of Iraqis volunteered to march to Israel to fight for their fellow Muslims.

Over the next few days, no specific threat against U.S. interests in the Middle East surfaced, but Americans in the region found the atmosphere very tense. There was an air of dread, a feeling that something terrible was going to happen. The U.S. State Department closed its embassies. The military was cautioned to "be alert."

USCENTCOM issues four levels of alert for its troops. Condition Alpha indicates that there is a general threat in the area, one that is unpredictable and indefinite. It's a "wait and see" status. Condition Bravo is issued when an attack of some kind is likely, even probable. The troops continue to operate as usual but work at a higher level of watchfulness. Condition Charlie means that an attack or an incidence of violence is about to happen. The troops are ordered to be armed and ready for combat. When an attack begins, Condition Delta is declared and retaliation is under way—troops fight back.

The USS *Cole* traveled into the Red Sea in early October at Threat Condition Bravo. Its major concern was not the situation in Israel, but where the ship's next fuel stop would be.

For years the navy had used the port of Djibouti for refueling its ships. That tiny African nation is located at the entrance to the Gulf of Aden, across the Red Sea from Yemen. Because of the number of vessels in the port, the wait in line to get service had grown to about twenty-four hours. It could take as long as twenty-four hours to fill up a ship the size of the *Cole* there. Spending two days at Djibouti was too long. When naval personnel reported that the fuel was dirty and not up to their standard, the Department of Defense decided to find an alternate refueling station.

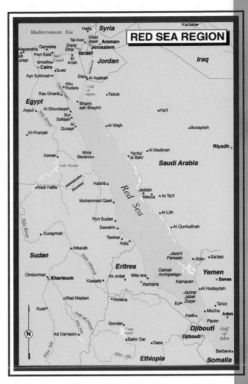

The Middle East, a politically unstable area that contains many valuable resources needed by the United States, has long been a region of conflict.

Aden, on the coast of Yemen, was a perfect location, halfway between the Suez Canal and the Persian Gulf. The port of Aden had been closed to U.S. military vehicles from 1969 to 1997, as the government shifted from militant to moderate. In 1998, USCENTCOM officials investigated the port and judged that it would be safe for naval vessels. There was no reason to believe that it would be more dangerous than Djibouti. Djibouti was frequently in turmoil because of the war in nearby Ethiopia.

An Aden supplier gave the navy a good bid, and a contract was signed. As part of the preparation for making the port suitable for U.S. ships, surveillance cameras were installed.

U.S. soldiers suit up in Fort Hood, Texas. They joined other troops in Kuwait as part of an operation code-named Desert Spring. After the Gulf War, the United States thought it best to maintain about 6,000 troops in the area to protect U.S. interests.

At a congressional hearing on October 25, 2000, some members of Congress questioned whether the contract with Aden was a political move: Did the State Department want to bring U.S. dollars to Yemen to make it an ally? General Franks replied that the State Department had absolutely no say in the choice. It was strictly a logistics decision. Aden was in the right location and was easily accessible to ships. If refueling there helped Yemen's economy, that was beside the point.

Other members of Congress asked why U.S. ships needed to use foreign ports at all for refueling. Why couldn't the navy use U.S. tankers and refuel at sea? Military officials pointed out that this is a very impractical solution. The cost would be staggering, and the procedure is time-consuming, difficult, and dangerous. It would tie up the navy's resources, and the tankers themselves would need refueling.

Early in the morning of October 12, 2000, as the *Cole* proceeded to Aden, 21,790 U.S. forces—soldiers, sailors, air force personnel, and marines—were in the AOR. These troops, along with 27 ships and 214 aircraft, were involved in one of three operations: Southern Watch to enforce the no-fly zone over Iraq; Operation Desert Spring, "a forward presence" in Kuwait; and the Maritime Intercept Operation (MIO) that the *Cole* was joining.

The ship was expected to be in the port of Aden for four to six hours. No one would be allowed to get off. A Yemeni pilot would be allowed on board to give instructions for maneuvering in the bay. As the *Cole* approached the fueling station, it was still at Threat Condition Bravo. Commander Lippold had not received word that any sort of attack, on either land or sea, was aimed at U.S. troops. There was not a hint of trouble in the bay.

At that time, the navy did not use a "pre-deploy" security force as it approached a port, as the U.S. Air Force did. Such an advance party could look the situation over and decide whether or not it was safe to proceed. If there had been a navy advance party, it would have judged the port of Aden safe on the morning of October 12.

Routine precautions for a naval vessel entering a high-threat area are listed in the "Procedures for Anti-Terrorism," a

General Tommy Franks answers questions for reporters. He has had a long military career and is now in charge of Operation Enduring Freedom.

manual issued by the Joint Forces staff to all branches of the U.S. military. They include adding highly visible armed sentries, posting signs in both English and the local language to warn small craft to remain clear, rigging fire hoses to repel small boats, and creating a protective picket line around the ship using the ship's small boats to keep unauthorized small craft away.

None of these precautions were taken because a specific threat had not been made. But another precaution was: The commander ordered all below-deck hatches "closed and dogged." This meant the doors between com-partments (or rooms) were closed and latched, preventing access from one compartment to another.

Four sailors stood watch topside as service boats skimmed the harbor. The sentries carried unloaded weapons— a safety precaution—but they were trained to load and fire in six seconds, as fast as humanly possible. General Franks reported what happened next in military style: "She was moored to the starboard side of the refueling dolphin [floating dock] at 0849 Yemen time. At 1000, the refueling alignment was verified and, at 1031, refueling operations began."

At 1400, Captain Lippold expected that the ship would be fueled up and headed toward the Arabian Sea.

Even though the USS *Cole* is one of the most heavily armored ships in the U.S. fleet, it was nearly destroyed by a few terrorists.

THE ATTACK

As the *Cole* tied up for fueling in Aden harbor on Columbus Day morning, crew members secured its huge mooring lines to the anchored buoys they called dolphins. These dolphins served as floating refueling docks. A dozen small boats puttered around the harbor. It was already hot, maybe ninety-five degrees Fahrenheit (thirty-five degrees Celsius), and the crew working below deck was grateful to have air-conditioning.

The city of Aden, surrounded by craggy volcanic hills, spread out before them. The sun glinted off the water. It seemed a peaceful scene. A few crew members, acting like tourists, took pictures.

Shortly before 11:30 AM, a small boat approached the *Cole*'s port side. It looked to be a twenty-foot fiberglass harbor tender. Two young men in the boat hailed the ship. The sentries thought they were offering to haul off the ship's garbage. Similar boats work as trash haulers in all ports.

At the same time, life below deck was routine. Petty Officer 1st Class John Washak moved into the lunch line on the mess deck, where fajitas were being served. Sonar technician Jennifer Kudrik was discussing chemical warfare with her supervisor in her office. Seaman Carl Wingate was taking a nap in his bunk. Chief Gunner's Mate Norman Larson, on his way to the ship's mess for lunch, saw the long food line and turned back to work on the paperwork on his desk. Lt. Ann Chamberlain, the ship's navigator, was working on a PowerPoint brief for the next leg of the journey. *Mission: Impossible* was playing on the video monitor in the mess room.

Suddenly there was a tremendous explosion. The ship lurched and shook, rose up about 15 feet (about 4.5 meters), and slammed back down.

An enormous load of explosives had been detonated. The explosion immediately tore a 40-by-40-foot (12-by-12-meter) hole through the half-inch steel of the hull and burst through an engine room, the mess deck, the chiefs' mess, and the galley. A torrent of steel, water, and flame followed. Ruptured hoses spewed hot fuel everywhere. The sounds of Klaxons and sirens mingled with the screams of the wounded.

This photo of the inside of the *Cole* was taken shortly after the attack. Even with damage this severe, the ship was able to return to active service.

Reacting automatically as they had been trained—even though they didn't yet know what had happened—the sentries on the top deck jumped onto the fueling pier. With guns drawn, they shouted "Hands up!" to the Yemeni working on the pier. The Yemeni obeyed at once, but through desperate gestures got the sentries to turn off the fuel nozzles before the gushing fuel burst into flame.

Aboard the ship was chaos. There were two immediate objectives: to keep the ship afloat and to help the injured. High-tech retaliation was forgotten—there was nothing left of the small boat or its occupants anyway.

Months of extensive planning went into the attack on the USS *Cole*. Because Yemen has no coast guard patrolling its 2,000 miles of coastline, there was no one to intercept the terrorists before they could carry out their plan.

The Ship

Water poured into the hole in the hull. Electrical generators had been hit and the lights went out, along with fans and the air-conditioning. Bare wires sparked before dying, threatening to ignite the fuel. Maintenance personnel scrambled to find flashlights, fire extinguishers, and portable pumps. With the ship's internal communication systems disabled, officers had to shout orders to the crew, adding to the noise and confusion.

In the dark, the extent of destruction was hard to gauge, and damage reports were slow in coming. It was clear that the mess decks and galley had been destroyed and that that was where most of the casualties would be found. In one area where the upper deck collapsed, the floor and ceiling had almost met, with only a few inches separating them.

One of the two main engine rooms had been all but destroyed. The huge three-story room was rapidly filling with seawater. Pumps were unable to keep up with it, and the ship seemed in danger of sinking. Within minutes of the explosion, the *Cole* had taken on 1,000 tons (907 metric tons) of water and was listing four degrees to port.

> When the explosion occurred, the immediate actions of the crew saved the ship and saved the lives of many, many of the crew members on board. The courageousness that was shown by them was unbelievable. They have worked non-stop since then. You can be proud of every single sailor on this ship.
>
> —Cmdr. Kirk Lippold, commanding officer, USS *Cole*, in an e-mail message to the families of crew members

The closed and dogged hatches kept the ship from sinking. This routine procedure saved hundreds of lives and saved the ship as well. Commander Lippold declared "Material Condition Zebra," and the sailors responded as they had been drilled, shutting all watertight doors on the ship to prevent further flooding. Some sailors were assigned to keep a constant vigil for leaks.

The Casualties

The casualties were horrible. Some people had been blown apart. Some were impaled on huge shards of metal or glass.

> **B**ravery came in many forms that day. We had fighting sailors on board the *Cole*, not men or women.
>
> —Lt. Commander Peterschmidt in a letter to the editor of the *Virginia Pilot* in response to criticism that women didn't perform well in combat

Many had multiple fractures and many were badly burned. All needed immediate care. Eight men were trapped under the mangled doors of the mess hall. Seven were rescued alive.

Neither the ship nor the crew was prepared for this kind of medical emergency. Hospital corpswoman Tayinikia Campbell set up an improvised triage area in the passageway from the mess deck, where the wounded were carried. After checking each one over, she called out instructions to volunteers on how to take care of them.

Sailor Carl Wingate knew first aid and went to work at once in the "Bloody Aisle," as the passageway was called. The moans and screams of the wounded were so loud, he could hardly hear or be heard when he asked them, "Where do you hurt the most?" He came upon a friend with both legs broken. Hollering for splints, he was handed a broom. He snapped it in half and made a splint for each leg, securing them with strips ripped from a shirt. As he moved down the line, he applied tourniquets made from belts. Others used the cardboard backing from desk calendars for makeshift splints. There was no access to appropriate medical supplies.

Thick, acrid smoke surrounded the survivors as they struggled to get the wounded up the stairs to the top deck and fresh air. Rescue workers breathed through their shirts, trying not to take in vapor from the spilled fuel. A few located gas masks.

Yemini marine ambulances responded quickly and took the wounded to a nearby hospital. The dead, seventeen in all, were put in a shed near where the *Cole* was moored. Some of the dead had been dismembered, blown apart by the bomb. Only six bodies were brought out on the first day. Several sailors in the engine room drowned before they could get out. Their bodies were caught in the twisted machinery and were unreachable.

The force of the explosion blew some sailors out of the ship into the gulf. Others, fearing fire, jumped. All were rescued by crew members.

Meanwhile, while the crew was trying to rescue their own, the hole in the side of the ship gaped large enough for a convoy of trucks to drive through.

Navy divers participated in the effort to salvage material from the USS *Cole*. Examining pieces of wreckage can provide experts with valuable information about the kind of explosives used in the attack.

THE AFTERMATH

It took a grueling seventy-two hours to stabilize the ship. Once they had escaped the horrors below deck, crew members were afraid to go back down. They caught catnaps on deck in the blazing sun between stints below and took turns sleeping at night. Without their searchlights, no one could see in the waters around the ships. They felt they were sitting ducks, helpless and exposed. All sounds were magnified. What if terrorists struck again?

Because the kitchen facilities had been destroyed by the blast, the crew had no food during this time except the snacks they kept in their own quarters. The U.S. Embassy ordered food from Yemeni hotels to be brought to the crew, but no one would accept it, fearing that it might be poisoned.

With the electricity out, the water pressure in the plumbing went to zero. The showers and toilets didn't work. Everyone was filthy, covered with fuel, blood, and the soot that settled on everything. Many were numb with shock and worked on autopilot. Diarrhea took hold of the crew because there was no clean water to drink.

Military Response

Washington was notified of the attack immediately. Within minutes of the news reaching the Pentagon, all ships in the AOR were raised to Condition Charlie. The Joint Task Force declared "Operation Determined Response."

According to his aides, President Bill Clinton was "seething." However, he did not want to jeopardize the volatile situation in Israel, so he kept his remarks formal and sent sympathetic and encouraging messages to the crew. The State Department and Congress agreed that it was impossible for the U.S. government to retaliate when no one knew who the culprit was. The Yemeni government expressed its innocence and promised support for the United States. To attack Yemen would do nothing but make more enemies.

Within hours of the explosion, USCENTCOM dispatched military units to Aden, and they continued to arrive over the next few days. Navy SEALs were first. They dropped to the ship from helicopters to look for evidence of terrorist sabotage and time-delayed weapons. They found none, but the crew was further frightened by the thought of more danger.

President Clinton attends a memorial service honoring those who died in the explosion.

The frigate USS *Hawes* and the destroyer USS *Donald Cook* were the closest to the *Cole*. When they arrived, morale went up on the crippled ship. Fellow sailors provided needed food, medical attention, laundry services, extra bunks, and other essential equipment. Navy divers stationed in Bahrain came aboard the *Cole* and disappeared into the flooded compartments for hours at a time. Some were trying to extricate bodies; others worked to make the ship's structure more stable.

Two Fleet Antiterrorism Security Teams (FAST) of U.S. Marines arrived in Aden with the mission to protect American interests, especially the U.S. Embassy. They had little to do with the *Cole*, but they gave the crew a sense of security. More marines arrived in the bay on three ships, part of the amphibious ready group. Their immediate job was to wait and watch. Other rescue crews joined the Americans— a French medical team and a British Royal Navy vessel.

When the U.S. Air Force transport arrived, thirty-three of the thirty-nine injured were flown from Aden hospitals to Landstuhl Regional Medical Center in Germany, an American military hospital. As soon as was medically advisable, they were transferred from there to the Portsmouth Naval Hospital in Norfolk, Virginia. Seeing the sudden grisly deaths of friends horrified the crew. A brief onboard funeral service helped to soften their loss. E-mail communication with relatives back home via the operational computers also helped to ease their shock and sorrow. In spite of the desperate conditions on board the ship and the opportunities to get on board another American ship, not a single crew member would leave the *Cole*.

Staying Afloat

Chief Engineer Deborah Courtney and her crew of engineers worked around the clock for nearly four days to isolate exposed electrical cables that threatened to ignite the fuel-soaked interior. They frequently had to wear oxygen masks in order to breathe, and that added to the danger. Maintenance people sprayed flame retardant foam everywhere they could reach.

As important as preventing fire was stopping the flooding. An emergency generator kept the pumps working at first, but they couldn't keep up with the rising water. When the generator went out, things seemed hopeless. But instead of abandoning ship, the entire crew formed an old-fashioned bucket brigade in the steaming, dark aisleways and worked for a full day to keep the ship afloat.

Using materials at hand, sailors aboard the *Cole* plugged up holes near the ship's propeller to prevent water from pouring in.

The pumps were started again, but it was obvious that they weren't powerful enough to take the water up three stories to the waterline. In desperation, engineers cut a hole in the side of the ship, allowing the pumps to empty at a lower level. It worked, and the ship was stabilized.

Going Home

Once the dead and injured were taken care of and the ship was stabilized, arrangements were made to return the ship to its home port in Virginia. The navy engaged the *Blue Marlin*, a Norwegian transport ship then in the port of Dubai, across the Arabian Peninsula from Aden in the Persian Gulf. It took more than a week for it to reach the *Cole*.

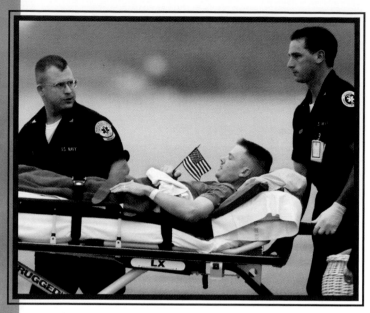

On his way to receive treatment, a sailor from the *Cole* holds a U.S. flag while being carried off of a plane.

Before the *Cole* could be transported, structural engineers made a careful study of the ship to prevent further damage when it was lifted aboard the *Blue Marlin*. Supporting pieces for the keel and the sides had to be constructed and placed. The physical characteristics of the *Cole* had been changed by the bomb blast, the weight on board redistributed, and the supports altered. When a building is hit by an explosion, its support structure may be so damaged that the building is unsalvageable and must be demolished. This was the fear for the *Cole.*

In all, about 5,000 government personnel were sent to Aden to rescue the *Cole*, provide security, and get the ship back home. An engineering assessment team from Naval Sea Systems Command evaluated the damage. To no one's surprise, they found the most serious damage in the engineering space. After several days of evaluation, they gave the go-ahead for the ship's transport home, and the 216 surviving sailors were evacuated.

On October 29, the Sealift Command's ocean tug, the USS *Catawba*, towed the *Cole* out of Aden Harbor into deeper

The USS *Cole* is brought into port on the back of a Norwegian heavy transport ship. It cost the United States $250 million to make the *Cole* operational again.

water. To load the *Cole* onto the transport ship required a water depth of at least 75 feet (approximately 23 meters), since it involved partially submerging the *Blue Marlin* and maneuvering the *Cole* into position over the *Blue Marlin*'s deck. The transport ship was then raised and the *Cole* was lifted aboard. It then had to be tilted on the *Blue Marlin*'s deck to protect the propellers and sonar dome.

At last the shattered *Cole* began its journey home.

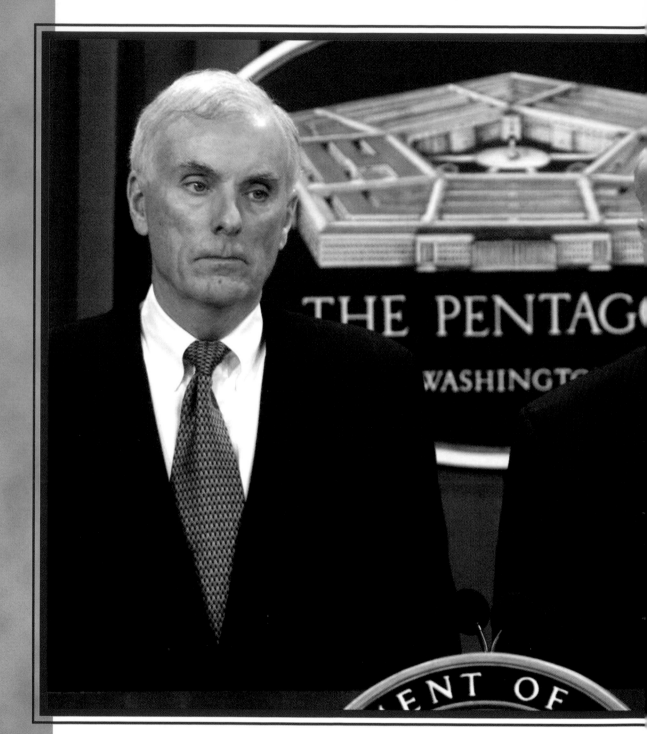

Speaking from inside the Pentagon, retired army general William Couch *(right)* and retired navy admiral Harold Gehman *(left)* discuss the bombing of the USS *Cole* with reporters.

THE INVESTIGATION

CHAPTER 5

While smoke from the explosion of the USS *Cole* still hung in the air, a clamor began in the United States and abroad to find out who did it, how they did it, and why they did it. A Yemeni police inquiry began at once, even before U.S. officials converged on the site.

It was 6:30 AM in Washington, D.C., when the White House notified Dale Watson, head of the FBI's Counter-Terrorism Division, of the explosion. He called the bureau's high-tech Strategic Operations and Information Center and the Critical Incident Response Group. They were ordered to get the rapid deployment team to Andrews Air Force Base outside Washington. A plane would be waiting to take them to Yemen.

Counterterrorism units from the FBI, the CIA, and the White House met to map strategy. *Time* magazine called this high-tech elite group "Terror Hunters." Right away they decided that the *Cole* attack had been planned by a small group of terrorists with international support and sophisticated bomb-making expertise.

The Criminal Investigation

The first FBI investigators, already in the AOR, arrived in Aden four hours after the explosion. They found out that the port's surveillance cameras were no longer in place. Local authorities said the police had not taken them. They had just "disappeared." That was a major disappointment and the first clue that the investigation would not be easy.

FBI agents continued to arrive for the next thirty hours and fanned out over the Arabian Peninsula, questioning people, following leads, and collecting information. A week after the explosion, FBI and U.S. Navy divers set up a crime-scene grid on the bottom of Aden Harbor to sift systematically for evidence. The divers searched inch by inch for the remains of the bomb, the boat that carried it, and the suicide bombers. All they found of the bombers were some teeth.

FBI agents confiscated the film used by the sailors who had been taking photos of the harbor as the boat approached. They questioned the Yemeni harbor pilot who had been aboard the ship. They were convinced he knew nothing about the bomb.

The president of Yemen, Ali Abdullah Saleh, stated the explosion could have been an accident. He said there was no proof that terrorists were involved. He soon changed his mind. On November 1, U.S. and Yemeni officials announced jointly that they had determined the type of bomb used on the *Cole*. It was C-4, a powerful plastic explosive containing RDX and

Ali Abdullah Saleh has been praised by President George W. Bush for his efforts to seek out and apprehend the terrorists responsible for the USS *Cole* bombing.

manufactured only in the United States, Austria, Iran, and a few other countries. Hundreds of pounds of C-4 had been used in the bomb.

Next, the Yemeni prime minister, Abdul Karim al-Ariani, admitted that Yemeni citizens had helped the bombers to falsify their identity cards. That raised questions about what other help was given. Yemeni police believed that at least five people were involved in the actual construction and deployment of the *Cole* bomb.

A break came when a twelve-year-old boy told Yemeni police that two men gave him the equivalent of $12

> **Y**ou are on notice. Our search for you will be relentless.
>
> —Secretary of Defense William Cohen's public warning to the killers at the memorial service for the fallen sailors

in Yemeni rials to watch their car. They had never returned for it. It was still where they left it, bearing license plates stolen in Yemen's hinterlands and loaded with diving gear and what seemed to be bomb equipment. The FBI impounded the car, angering Yemeni officials.

Information surfaced that the men may have had as many as five safe houses as they moved around the community preparing the bomb and the boat. Neighbors at one location remembered two men working on a boat, using welding equipment. At another location, a more secluded house in an exclusive neighborhood, investigators found bomb-making equipment.

As the months went on, tension increased between U.S. and local investigators. Yemeni officials refused to allow the FBI to join local police on their searches or in interviews with suspects. Unless they could be a part of the investigation, the FBI insisted, the United States wouldn't accept the Yemeni findings as valid.

The FBI stopped their investigation in June 2001 because Ambassador Barbara Bodine refused to give them permission to carry heavy weapons, or, as an FBI spokesperson said, "to arm themselves appropriately." Bodine was trying to prevent problems with the Yemeni government officials, who felt the overzealous Americans were being high-handed. She stated that FBI investigators would be protected by the same diplomatic security rules as were agents who guard U.S. diplomats at the U.S. Embassy.

At the end of August 2001, officials of both countries reached an agreement and the FBI returned to Yemen.

Barbara Bodine, the U.S. ambassador to Yemen at the time of the USS *Cole* incident, told the international press, "We persisted and we survived. What was good was being able to see how human nature can endure."

Other Investigations

Congress convened a hearing on the *Cole* disaster on October 25, 2000. Its investigation was concerned with what USCENTCOM and NAVCENT had done wrong (or right) before, during, and after the attack. General Franks, State Department officials, and Defense Department officials testified in both public and closed session. The result was a recommendation for higher security levels for vessels in the AOR. There was also a strong suggestion for better medical preparation on ships.

Commonly believed to be the mastermind behind the September 11, 2001, attacks on the United States, Osama bin Laden has been wanted by the U.S. government since 1998, when he carried out the bombing of the U.S. Embassies in Kenya and Tanzania.

The Naval Criminal Investigative Service under Admiral Robert J. Natter, chief of the Atlantic Fleet, made a report evaluating the role of navy personnel in responding to the disaster. This report, issued in January 2002, stated that Commander Lippold "acted reasonably in adjusting his force protection."

A major recommendation of the report was that "the Navy needs to do a better job of both training and equipping its ships to operate with reasonable risk in a high-threat environment."

On October 2, 2001, three weeks after the attacks on the World Trade Center and the Pentagon, U.S. officials

Mohammed Hamdi Al-Ahdal (*top*) and Qaed Sunian Al-Harethi (*bottom*) were wanted by the U.S. and Yemeni governments in connection with the bombing of the USS *Cole*. Both men forged links to Al Qaeda when fighting against Soviet forces in Afghanistan in the 1980s.

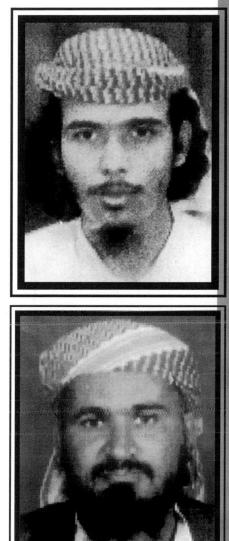

tied together the 1998 embassy bombings in Tanzania and Kenya and the attack on the *Cole*. They had found telephone and bank records that spelled out a link between Osama bin Laden's Al Qaeda network and all these bombings. Later, a surveillance tape came to light that showed one of the suspected September 11 hijackers meeting in Kuala Lumpur, Malaysia, with a man suspected in the bombing of the *Cole*.

Yemeni officials agreed that Osama bin Laden was behind the bombing. On February 5, 2002, Saleh, Yemen's president, announced that his security forces were seeking two top Al Qaeda operatives in connection with the *Cole* bombing. The men were identified as Mohammed Hamdi Al-Ahdal, also known as Abu Assem, and Qaed Sunian Al-Harethi, also known as Abu Ali.

All they had to do was find them.

Palestinian children march in support of Hamas, an organization that wants to set up a government in the land originally known as Palestine. Since 1948, most of this land has been contained by Israeli borders.

THE TERRORISTS

Yemen is one of the poorest nations in the AOR. Its statistics make it a fertile ground for terrorist groups to recruit new members. United Nations figures show that almost 50 percent of the population is under the age of fifteen. The average family has 7.6 children, and 60 percent of these families scrape a living from agriculture, mainly sheep raising, in an arid land with rocky soil. The infant mortality rate is high; life expectancy is under sixty years. Education is spotty and limited. Only 13 percent of Yemeni girls go to school at all. The estimated unemployment rate is 30 percent.

Yemen is an ancient country. Two thousand years ago it supplied world markets with such exotic items as frankincense, myrrh, spices, and condiments. For hundreds of years, Yemen was closed to the outside world, but it is now re-opening its doors to trade, hoping to join the global marketplace.

Yemen shares a long border with Saudi Arabia. Attempts at regulating and patrolling the border have caused a longstanding dispute between the two countries. Yemen controls the eastern side of the Bab el Mandeb choke point at the southern end of the Red Sea, which is considered a strategic location. The port of Aden is 1,400 miles south of Suez and 1,400 miles southwest of the Strait of Hormuz, which connects the Persian Gulf and the Gulf of Oman.

In the early 1990s, a civil war racked the nation, making economic growth impossible. The United States cut off its foreign aid for Yemen when the country openly supported Saddam Hussein during Operation Desert Storm in 1991.

The Yemeni government was unified in 1994 with a new constitution. Islamic law is the basis of all its legislation, and the philosophy of the government is socialist. Women were given the vote in 1993, but the education of women is not encouraged.

The Muslim Connection

Islam is one of the world's great religions. There are many varieties of Islam, just as there are many varieties of Christianity,

Judaism, Hinduism, and Buddhism. Only a small proportion of Muslims are extremist, but it is this group that the world is focusing on because of their support for violent acts.

With an Islamic Jihad flag held out in front of him, an Islamic Jihad soldier marches at a funeral for a fellow soldier, who was killed in a clash with Israeli forces.

Yemen is a Muslim nation, but not all its Muslims are extremists. Some of the varieties of Islam in Yemen are Sunni, Shafi'i, Shiite, and Zaydi. Within these groups are the full range of adherents, from fanatic to lukewarm.

Muslim fundamentalism as it is emerging today is both anti-Western and antimodern. Fundamentalists see the subservient role of women as crucial to a healthy society. They go to great lengths to control women by isolating them and controlling how they look and what they do. Western ideas that women should be free to choose their own destiny and act as full partners in a marriage seem evil to them. They want to destroy the means of spreading these ideas, such as Western movies, television, books, and magazines. Democracy, with its emphasis on equality of all people, is also considered evil.

The struggle against evil is called a holy war, a jihad. It is a battle that all religious people wage, but each religious group has its own definition of evil. In Islam, it is considered a Muslim duty to conduct a jihad. There are four methods to use: the heart, the tongue, the hand, and the sword. The first three are familiar to other faiths—to do good by word and action. The fourth seems unique to Islam today, although some extremist Christians also believe in using "the sword"—or a bomb—to dispose of their enemies. Most Muslims are forbidden from participating in hostile acts; only a small percentage of them have made it a part of their faith.

Religious or ideological terrorist groups, whether Christian, Muslim, Maoist, or anything else, are especially dangerous because they see political issues as "good vs. evil," with no middle ground. They aim to destroy the opposition, not to negotiate with it or accommodate it. When extremists perceive that God asks them to die for a cause, they do so gladly, expecting to be rewarded in heaven or paradise.

Several extremist groups are known to be in Yemen. Some are native groups and others have come from Saudi Arabia or other nearby countries. The avowedly terrorist groups Hamas and the Palestinian Islamic Jihad are recognized as legal organizations in Yemen and maintain offices there. Other groups are in Yemen without state endorsement and are considered illegal: the Egyptian Islamic Jihad, a-Gama'a al-Islamiya, the Algerian Armed Islamic Group, various Libyan groups, and Al Qaeda, the group masterminded by Osama bin Laden.

Sitting on a bench in the Tora Bora Mountains, captured Al Qaeda fighters are lined up in front of the media. They had been holed up in Al Qaeda's last stronghold in the Tora Bora Mountains before their capture.

Three groups immediately claimed responsibility for the attack on the *Cole*: the Islamic Army of Aden, Muhammad's Army, and the Islamic Deterrence Force. It is known now that none of these actually planned or executed the bombing, but all gave moral support to it. The group really responsible is Al Qaeda.

Osama bin Laden has a strong influence in the AOR. Young people listen carefully to his speeches, watch his videos, and believe his promise that their lives will be better once the West is destroyed. In 1996, bin Laden issued a fatwa against the United States. This religious ruling urged Muslims to kill Americans. He trains mujahideen, Muslim holy warriors, to carry out violent acts against the people he labels the enemy. He is believed to be the mastermind behind the attacks on the U.S. Embassies in Kenya and Tanzania in 1998, which killed more than 200 people, as well as the attacks on the *Cole*, the World Trade Center, and the Pentagon.

The terrorist cells he inspires are not actually physically connected to him. They may keep in touch through the Internet, but they don't meet with him in person. The idea is to keep the structure of Al Qaeda and similar organizations very loose. Small groups are often made up of family members or longtime friends. They build an intense loyalty to each other and make pacts to die together. There is no chain of command to satisfy, so they are free to follow through with any idea that comes to them. Al Qaeda can supply them with the materials they need.

Terrorist cells are spread out geographically, which gives them much more security than if they met in a central location. These cells are very difficult to locate because the members seem like normal householders and shopkeepers. They don't wear uniforms or act suspiciously. They can move to a new location quickly and can cross national boundaries if necessary. Like-minded groups are willing to hide them or provide them with new identities.

So far, counterterrorist units have not been able to keep up with them. The evidence for that is in the story of the *Cole*: A homemade bomb nearly sank a billion-dollar ship carrying the most sophisticated weaponry in the world.

THOSE WHO DIED

- Hull Maintenance Technician 2nd Class **Kenneth Eugene Clodfelter**, 21, Mechanicsville, VA

- Electronics Technician **Richard Costelow**, 35, Morrisville, PA

- Mess Management Specialist Seaman **Lakeina Monique Francis**, 19, Woodleaf, NC

Kenneth Eugene Clodfelter
Hull Maintenance Technician 3rd Class

Lakeina Monique Francis
Mess Management Specialist Seaman

Timothy Lee Gauna
Info. Systems Technician Seaman

Marc Ian Nieto
Engineman 2nd Class

Ronald Scott Owens
Electronics Warfare Technician 3rd Class

Joshua Langdon Parlett
Engineman Fireman

Patrick Howard Roy
Fireman Apprentice

Kevin Shawn Rux
Electronics Warfare Technician 2nd Class

Ronchester Mananga Santiago
Mess Management Specialist 3rd Class

Gary Graham Swenchonis Jr.
Fireman

- Information Systems Technician **Timothy Lee Gauna**, 21, Rice, TX

- Signalman Seaman **Cherone Louis Gunn**, 22, Rex, GA

- Seaman **James Rodrick McDaniels**, 19, Norfolk, VA

- Engineman 2nd Class **Marc Ian Nieto**, 24, Fon du Lac, WI

- Electronics Warfare Technician **Ronald Scott Owens**, 24, Vero Beach, FL

- Seaman **Lakiba Nicole Palmer**, 22, San Diego, CA

- Engineman Fireman **Joshua Langdon Parlett**, 19, Churchville, MD

- Fireman Apprentice **Patrick Howard Roy**, 19, Hudson, NY

- Electronics Warfare Technician 1st Class **Kevin Shawn Rux**, 30, Portland, ND

- Mess Management Specialist 3rd Class **Ronchester Manangan Santiago**, 22, Kingsville, TX

- Operations Specialist 2nd Class **Timothy Lamont Saunders**, 32, Ringgold, VA

- Fireman **Gary Graham Swenchonis Jr.**, 26, Rockport, TX

- Ensign **Andrew Triplett**, 31, Macon, MS

- Seaman **Craig Bryan Wibberley**, 19, Williamsport, MD

A memorial in Norfolk, Virginia, was built to honor the sailors who died in the attack on the USS *Cole*. The memorial is located in the town of the ship's home port.

The Memorial

The first memorial service for the *Cole* was held at Pier 12 at the Norfolk Naval Station in Virginia on October 18, 2000. It honored the known dead and those still missing. Families of the victims, military officials, and other

Sailors stand at attention while the national anthem is played during a memorial service for the crew of the USS *Cole.*

government personnel attended, as well as President Clinton and Secretary of Defense William Cohen.

One year later, on October 12, 2001, only a month after the tragic events of September 11, friends and families of those on the *Cole* dedicated a monument to those who had fallen. Military personnel and civilians gathered at Norfolk to dedicate a ten-foot granite memorial overlooking Willoughby Bay. It has two bronze plaques listing the names of the seventeen dead sailors. Thousands of people throughout the country made contributions to the Navy-Marine Corps Relief Society fund to pay for the monument.

On April 19, 2002, the USS *Cole* returned to the sea. It had taken fourteen months and $250 million to repair the ship. It had been offloaded from the *Blue Marlin* on

On September 19, 2002, the USS *Cole* returned to duty after a send-off in Pascagoula, Mississippi. The ship spent over a year out of commission, receiving repairs and improvements.

December 13, 2000, into a predredged deepwater facility at the shipyard of Northrop Grumman Ship Systems, Ingalls Operations in Pascagoula, Mississippi. The navy decided to repair the ship rather than scrap it based on the costs involved. But the major reason the *Cole* was saved was that the crew—and many Americans—didn't want to give Osama bin Laden and other terrorists the satisfaction of thinking they had won. The message they wanted to send to him was, "We're going to fight back."

One of the additions to the refurbished ship was a passageway with seventeen white stars embedded in blue tile to memorialize those who were killed.

GLOSSARY

AOR (Area of Responsibility)   The twenty-five Middle Eastern countries that are monitored by U.S. intelligence.

C-4   A powerful plastic explosive frequently used by terrorists.

destroyer   Naval designation for a small, fast warship.

emplacement   A position for a military weapon.

extremist   A person who holds extreme positions in matters of religion and politics.

fatwa   A declaration made by a Muslim leader regarding proper Muslim behavior.

jihad   A religious war against evil.

NAVCENT   Naval Central Command in the AOR.

sanction   A coercive measure adopted usually by several nations acting together against a nation violating international law.

sentry   A guard.

sovereign   Describes a nation free from outside control.

triage   Sorting injured people for medical treatment.

USCENTCOM   U.S. Central Command that supervises the military forces in the AOR.

For More Information

Federal Bureau of Investigation
Department of Justice
935 Pennsylvania Avenue NW, Room 7972
Washington, DC 20535
(202) 324-3000
Web site: http://www.fbi.gov

Federal Emergency Management Agency
500 C Street SW
Washington, DC 20472
(202) 566-1600
Web site: http://www.fema.gov

U.S. Department of Defense
1400 Defense Pentagon, Room 3A750
Washington, DC 20301-1400
(703) 428-0711
Web site: http://www.defenselink.mil

U.S. Department of Justice
950 Pennsylvania Avenue NW
Washington, DC 20530-0001
(202) 353-1555
Web site: http://www.usdoj.gov

U.S. Department of State
2201 C Street NW
Washington, DC 20520
(202) 647-4000
Web site: http://www.state.gov

Web Sites

Due to the changing nature of Internet links, the Rosen Publishing Group, Inc., has developed an online list of Web sites related to the subject of this book. This site is updated regularly. Please use this link to access the list:

http://www.rosenlinks.com/ta/ussc/

FOR FURTHER READING

Baer, Robert. *See No Evil: The True Story of a Ground Soldier in the CIA's War on Terrorism.* New York: Crown, 2002.

Gaines, Ann. *The Navy in Action.* Springfield, NJ: Enslow Publishers, 2001.

Gaines, Ann G. *Terrorism.* Philadelphia: Chelsea House Publishers, 1999.

Maas, Peter. *Terrible Hours: The Man Behind the Greatest Submarine Rescue in History.* New York: HarperCollins, 1999.

Marsh, Carole. *United We Stand: America's War Against Terrorism.* Atlanta: Gallopade Publishing Group, 2001.

Newcomb, Richard F., and Peter Maas. *Abandon Ship! The Saga of the USS Indianapolis, the Navy's Greatest Sea Disaster.* New York: HarperCollins, 2000.

Reeve, Simon. *The New Jackals.* Boston: Northeastern University Press, 1999.

BIBLIOGRAPHY

Bartholet, Jeffrey, et al. "A Sneak Attack." *Newsweek*, October 23, 2000.

Department of Defense. News Briefing, October 17, 2000. Retrieved May 2002 (http://defenselink.mil/news/Oct2000/t10172000t1017asd.html).

Department of Defense. USS *Cole* Commission Report, Executive Summary, January 9, 2001. Retrieved April 2002 (http://www.defenselink.mil/pubs/*cole*20010109.html).

Ehrenberg, Steven. "Who Is Osama bin Laden?" Scholastic On-Line Special Reports. Retrieved April 2002 (http://teacher.scholastic.com/newszone/specialreports/under_attack/suspect.htm).

Newman, Richard J. "Saving a Crippled Ship." U.S. News Online. October 20, 2000. Retrieved May 2002 (http://www.usnews/news/001030/ship.htm).

Thomas, Evan, and Sharon Squassoni. "Desperate Hours." *Newsweek*, October 23, 2000.

United States Congress, House Committee on Armed Services. The Attack on the U.S.S. *Cole*: Hearing, October 25, 2000. Washington: GPO.

White, Michael. "The New Terrorism." Annual report of the Stephen Roth Institute for the Study of Contemporary Anti-Semitism and Racism, 2000–2001.

Wingate, Carl. "The Bloody Aisle." ABCNews.com. January 18, 2001. Retrieved March 2002 (http://www.abcnews.go.co/sections/primetime/2020/PRIMETIMEusscolfeature.hmtl).

INDEX

About the Author

Betty Burnett is a freelance writer who lives in St. Louis, Missouri.

Photo Credits

Cover, pp. 22–23, 25, 30–31, 33 © AFP/Corbis; pp. 6–7, 11, 12, 18, 20, 26, 37, 38–39, 41, 43, 44, 45, 46–47, 49, 53, 54, 56 © AP/Wide World Photos; pp. 14–15, 35, 36, 51 © Reuters NewMedia Inc./Corbis; p. 17 © Maps.com/Corbis; p. 55 courtesy of the U.S. Navy.

Editor

Christine Poolos

Series Design and Layout

Geri Giordano